Franklin Family History

From 1425 England to 2018 U.S.A.

FRANKLIN

William M. Franklin

Franklin Family History: From 1425 England to 2018 U.S.A.

Copyright © 2018 William M. Franklin

Published by Thomas-Jacob Publishing, LLC
TJPub@thomas-jacobpublishing.com

Library of Congress Control Number: 2018964313
1. Reference/Genealogy and Heraldry 2. Family and Relationships/Reference
ISBN-10: 0-9979517-7-X
ISBN-13: 978-0-9979517-7-6
Thomas-Jacob Publishing, LLC, Deltona, Florida

First Edition

First Printing: November 2018

Printed in the United States of America

Table of Contents

Acknowledgements

$\mathcal{F}$irst, before I begin with our history, I want to thank three people who worked very hard to make this possible. First, I want to thank my first cousin, Barbara Jean Franklin, daughter of John Franklin (deceased) who spent years researching the Franklin history in America. Second, I want to thank my son, William Michael Franklin, for accepting the challenge to research our history in England and determine who our ancestors were. Last, but certainly not least, I want to thank my daughter, Dr. Melinda Rae (Franklin) Clayton for her tireless effort in bringing to us many corrections and additional information about our ancestors. Her discovery of a third Robert in the chain allows for many corrections to be made to earlier research.

Important Note Regarding Corrections

Previous research has told us that there were only two Roberts in the initial years after our line of the Franklins reached American soil: Robert Franklin I and his son Robert Franklin II. In that research, Robert I was married twice, first to Sarah Puddington and then to Sarah Gott. This is incorrect. Robert I was married to Mary Puddington and remained married to her until he died in 1682. Mary died in 1705.

It was Robert II who married Sarah Gott. Robert II and Sarah had two children: Robert III and Sarah. Robert II died at about 29 years of age. Almost all that has previously been reported about Robert II actually belongs to Robert III.

Hall (1941) is one of our sources. Hall was unaware at the time of his extensive research that there were actually three direct generations of Robert instead of two. In fact, he often expressed confusion regarding conflicting information in the course of his own research of the Franklin family line. When we reference Hall in relation to events that happened to Robert III, it's important to know that in his writing, he believed those events happened to Robert II.

Because one Robert was left out of earlier research, many of the dates of birth, marriage, and death we had previously accepted are now proved incorrect, and in some cases, make no sense at all.

Introduction

When tracing family history, it can be difficult to know which path to follow, particularly when that history spans hundreds of years and two different continents. The matter is made even more complicated due to the simple fact that historically, women have taken on the surname of their husbands. That, combined with the reality that for centuries women weren't allowed to own land, work, or participate in government matters, can make finding detailed, documented information regarding our female ancestors quite difficult.

For these reasons, and to streamline the process as much as possible, we followed the surname Franklin from son to father all the way back to Robert Franklin, born in Skipton-upon-Craven, Yorkshire, England in 1425.

Along the way, we included as much information as we could find regarding wives, daughters, careers, and public service.

Although information for the Franklin family does exist before 1425, reliable sources for information such as births, dates, and in some cases even names, become too scarce for us to form a substantial link. The family tree at that point begins to look a little bare.

The name Franklin has been spelled several different ways through the generations; Frankeleyn, Francklyn, Frankland, and Francklin, are just a few of the variations. Although the name is spelled differently on various documents over the centuries, I'll use the modern spelling here in order to be consistent and alleviate any confusion.

Furthermore, the same family names are used repeatedly throughout the generations. When the same father, son, and occasionally grandson share the same name, I'll use I, II, and III to help erase confusion.

The information here is as accurate as we're able to make it. In some cases, dates of birth and death vary by a year or more, depending on the sources used. This occurred most often for the first two generations living in North America, likely because during those pre-colonial and early colonial years adequate methods for keeping such records were either not yet developed or were simply not preserved. In those cases, if we were unable to find a reliable source, we chose to use the date most frequently cited. We've included in-text citations for sourced information as well as a bibliography at the end of the book.

The Franklin Family in England

We'll begin our journey with Robert Franklin (1425-1492), who according to genealogist Bernard Burke (1858) was from Skipton-upon-Craven, Yorkshire, England.

Public family records on some online genealogy sites list his father as John Frankeleyn of Ebryrghton, date of birth unknown, date of death 1390. There is a John Frankeleyn listed as a scholar at King's Hall in 1379 (Venn & Venn, 1922). According to Venn and Venn, this John Frankeleyn did indeed die in 1390. Given our family history of vicars and rectors, this information certainly fits in with what we have. However, since our Robert was born in 1425 and this man died in 1390, he clearly isn't Robert's father.

Other public entries on various online genealogy sites indicate John of Ebryrghton is actually the grandfather of Robert. They list John of Ebryrghton's son as John II, born sometime around 1390 in Sobbury, Gloucestershire, England. On those entries, John II is identified as the father of Robert. While the dates work and it is certainly possible John II was born shortly before or after his father died, the entries we have come across are unsourced, and we are not able to corroborate this information outside of those sites.

What we do know, thanks to genealogist Bernard Burke (1858) and our other sources, is that we are directly descended from Robert Franklin. We know that he married, although we do not know his wife's name.

They had at least one child, a son named William. To alleviate confusion, I'll refer to him as William I.

———————————

William I was born in 1460. The date of his death

in the public family records on several online genealogy sites is 1556, but this is highly unlikely, because this would mean he was ninety-six years old at the time of his death. The average lifespan in England at that time was around thirty-five years (Lambert, 2018). It's possible his date of birth has been confused with that of one of his sons, also named William. William I, who according to some online public family records was sometimes referred to as Sir William of Bedford, England, was married to a woman named Margaret. Many of those same public family records refer to Margaret as Lady Margaret Bullock of Risby (1465-1543).

Burke (1858) refers to her as "Margaret, dau. [daughter] of Risly, of Ravensdon" (p. 411).

William I and Margaret had the following children:

- John I, born 1480 and died 1542. We are direct descendants of John I.

- Thomas, dates of birth and death unknown.
- Richard, dates of birth and death unknown.
- William II. William II's date of birth is listed in our sources as "about" 1480, and he died 1555-56. William was educated at Queens' College, Cambridge, and during his lifetime held positions as the President of Queens' College, the Ambassador to Scotland, the Dean of York, and the Dean of Durham. On December 17, 1536, William was appointed Dean of Windsor, spiritual head of the Canons of St George's Chapel at Windsor Castle, England (Burke, 1858; Burke, Burke, & Nichols, 1846; Cooper, 1861).

William I's son, John I (1480-1542), married Elizabeth Berry (1509-1560).

They had two children:

- Elizabeth, dates of birth and death unknown.

- John II. We have no information on the date of birth for John. Scanned pages compiling *Norfolk England Bishop's Transcripts 1579-1935*, available on Ancestry.com, tell us he died on May 15, but the scanned page doesn't include the year. We are direct descendants of John II.

John I's son, John II, was married twice. He first married a woman Burke (1858) describes as "Elizabeth, dau. [daughter] of Halle, of Mildham, co. Durham" (p. 411). They had three children:

- John III, dates of birth and death unknown.

- William, dates of birth and death unknown.

- Daughter, name unknown, dates of birth and death unknown.

John II's second wife was Anne Copley of Bedford (Burke, Burke, & Nichols, 1846). John II and Anne had three sons:

- Edward I, born 1548, died 1617. We are direct descendants of Edward I.
- George, dates of birth and death unknown.
- Thomas I, dates of birth and death unknown, but we do know that at various times in his life he served as Alderman of London (Beaven, 1908; Burke, 1858; Harleian Society, 1880). Thomas I married Alice, "... dau. [daughter] of Humphrey Brown, Esq. of London" (Burke, Burke, & Nichols, 1846, p. 443). Thomas I and Alice had two sons, Thomas II and George. Thomas II would eventually emigrate to North

America with his second cousin, Robert Franklin I.

John II's son, Edward I (1548-1617), was a rector in The Church of England, specifically of Hertford County, Kelshull, England. He was married to Rebecca Willett, who was the daughter of a rector in The Church of England (Burke, Burke, & Nichols, 1846). Edward I and Rebecca had three children:

- Elizabeth, dates of birth and death unknown.
- John, date of birth unknown, but he died in 1641 (Burke, Burke, & Nichols, 1846).
- Edward II, born 1586 and died 1644. We are direct descendants of Edward II.

Edward I's son Edward Franklin II was also a rector in the Church of England. Edward II was well educated, having received his B.A. from Christ College Cambridge in 1604, his M.A. in 1608, his Bachelor of Divinity in 1616, and his Doctor of Divinity in 1630 (Peile, 1910).

He was ordained as a priest in London in December 1610 at the age of 23. He first served as a chaplain to Lord Chancellor Bacon, then held the rectory of St. Laurance Dengie in 1620. From there, he was Rector of Little Cressingham, Norfolk from 1622-1627. His final place of service was as Rector of Great Cressingham from 1627 until shortly before his death in 1644 (Peile, 1910). The church in Great Cressingham, St. Michael's, was built in the 1300s and is still in service today.

Edward II was married to Elizabeth Montfort (1600-1677) on August 8, 1626. Elizabeth's father was also a rector in The Church of England (Burke, Burke, & Nichols, 1846).

Edward II and Elizabeth had five children. They were:

- John, born 1628, date of death unknown. John also became a rector

(Burke, Burke, & Nichols, 1846).

- Robert I, born 1630 and died 1682. We are direct descendants of Robert I.
- Rebecca, born 1630, date of death unknown.
- Edward III, born 1638, date of death unknown.
- Elizabeth, born 1640, date of death unknown.

I have on file copies of the baptism of two of Edward II's children. Edward III was baptized by his father July 8, 1638, and Elizabeth, the daughter, was baptized by her father April 7, 1640 (*London, England Church of England Baptisms, Marriages and Burials 1538-1812*).

The English Civil War (1642-1651) saw many traditionalist clergy ejected from their parishes and homes. According to McCall (2016), "Traditionalist clergy formed a significant group amongst those who supported the King's [Charles I] cause and were amongst the worst affected by his eventual defeat [in 1646].

The scale of clerical ejections was unprecedented, even compared to the Reformation, one of the main events of the Civil War period" (p. 4).

In an earlier work, "Scandalous and Malignant? Settling Scores Against the Leicestershire Clergy After the First Civil War," McCall states, "During and after the first civil war, as part of a sweeping programme of religious reform, the Long Parliament denounced, tried, and removed from their livings thousands of clergy deemed to be 'scandalous', 'malignant', or 'delinquent' in their behaviour. The scale of the ejections was huge, possibly even surpassing the successive clerical upheavals during the sixteenth-century Reformation" (2015). McCall (2015) goes into great detail regarding the questionable procedures that resulted in such mass ejections.

Edward II was one of the clergy who was ejected in this manner. According to John Walker, author of *Sufferings of the Clergy* (as cited by Peile, 1910), Edward was ejected from Great Cressingham in 1644 in spite of being "a man of strict piety and unblemished life" (p. 263). According to Peile (1910) he was "driven from place to place" (p. 263) until, according to Walker (as cited by Peile) "the place, where he was, being beset with soldiers he endeavoured to make his escape through a garden, but as he was getting over the pales one of them run into his groyn, of which he soon after died" (p. 263).

In spite of the upheaval and tragedy that befell the family during England's Civil War, Edward II's son, John, was admitted to Caius in 1646 and would also become a rector (Peile, 1910).

Edward II's son Robert (1630-1682) ultimately emigrated to North America.

The Franklin Family Arrives in America

According to Thomas John Hall III, in his book *Hall Family of West River and Kindred Families* (1941), Robert Franklin I came to the Province of Maryland from England in 1642. Mr. Hall states that he received all of his information on the Franklin family from the late J. Harris Franklin.

It's nearly impossible to document the precise date of the arrival of Robert I in America, but 1642 seems to be the date that has been accepted by the Franklin family in the generations since. The earliest record of Robert I's arrival by ship to America is 1667 (*U.S. and Canada, Passenger and Immigration Lists Index, 1500s-1900s*). However, there is ample information to prove Robert I was in America well before that date.

The family has always heard that Robert I came over from England with an older brother named Thomas. This is almost accurate. Robert I did not have a brother named Thomas, but he did have a second cousin named Thomas (Burke, 1858; Burke, Burke, & Nichols, 1846; Harleian Society, 1880). According to these sources, Thomas Franklin's father (Thomas Franklin I) and Robert I's grandfather (Edward Franklin I) were brothers, both descended from John Franklin II of Bedford.

Some sources indicate that Thomas II was in Maryland years before he was joined by Robert I. For example, according to Ancestry.com's Public Family Records, Thomas II married his first wife in Maryland in 1640. Information on that wife is scarce; all we can find is that her last name was Harvey. The accuracy of this information is questionable, and we're unable to verify it. If he was indeed married to a Harvey, we assume she died, because in 1643

Thomas II married Mary Neale in England (Burke, 1858; Burke, Burke, & Nichols, 1846; *Essex, England Select Church of England Parish Registers, 1518-1960*).

There are also records of a Thomas Franklin who was active in Maryland's General Assembly at St. Mary's as early as 1637 (Proceedings and Acts of the General Assembly January 1637/8-September 1664.), but there is not enough information from that source to determine if this was the Thomas Franklin from our specific family line.

At any rate, since Robert I would have been only 12 years old in 1642 (he was born in 1630), Thomas II most likely either sent for him or went back to get him in 1642, or perhaps brought him back with him in 1643 with his new wife. We will probably never know for sure.

Robert Franklin I in Anne Arundel County, Maryland

We know that Robert I began to purchase land just a few years after his arrival to Maryland. In 1659 he had patented to him 200 acres called Gordon, and in 1662 he had obtained 150 acres called Beaver Dam. Hall (1941) speculated that Robert I may have been squatting on the land known as Beaver Dam for years before officially acquiring it. In 1674 he had 300 more acres of Beaver Dam patented to him. By the time of his death in 1682, Robert I owned 1100 acres of ground (Browne and Dielman, 1906a; Browne and Dielman, 1906b).

When he was about 20 years old, Robert I married a young girl named Mary Puddington. Mary was probably only about 13 years old when she married. Mary was born around 1636 and died in 1705. She was the daughter of George and Mary Puddington (Papenfuse, Day, Jordan, & Stiverson, 2008). Mary immigrated to the U.S. from England with her parents and her sister, Comfort, in 1649 (*U.S. and Canada, Passenger and Immigration Lists Index, 1500s-1900s*).

Robert I and Mary had their one and only child, Robert II, in or about 1650. According to a scanned copy of the *London, England Church of England Baptisms, Marriages and Burials 1538-1812* available through Ancestry.com, Robert I and Mary Puddington returned to England in 1652 to have Robert II baptized in The Church of England.

Robert I returned to England at least one more time in 1667 when he went back to bring to Maryland three free adults (Papenfuse et al., 2008). Barbara Jean Franklin states in her research that according to Maryland State Archives researcher notes, it was William Stinson and Anne and Augustine Skinner who came with Robert from England in 1667. Anne Skinner was a cousin of Robert's.

For bringing these three from England, Robert I received rights to 200 acres of land (Papenfuse et al., 2008).

Robert I officially immigrated in 1664 (Papenfuse et al., 2008). Besides being a land owner, planter, and merchant, he served in the Lower House in Anne Arundel County from 1671 to 1675. He was a justice in Anne Arundel County from 1668 to 1679. He was also sheriff of Anne Arundel County from 1678 until his death in 1682 (Anne Arundel County Maryland Judicial Branch: Sheriffs, n.d.). Robert I was only 52 years old when he died.

Robert Franklin II in Anne Arundel County, Maryland

We know very little about Robert II (1650-1680). We know of his baptism in 1652, but know nothing else of him until his marriage in 1674 to Sarah Gott (1654-1702). Sarah had been married two times before, first to Alexander Gordon and then to John Ewens. Both husbands had died (Barnes, 2005). She had no children by her first two husbands. She and Robert II had two children:

- Robert III, born in 1675 and died in 1730.

- Sarah, dates of birth and death unknown.

The next thing we know about Robert II is that in 1676 William Collier in his will left to

Robert II two cows, a feather bed, furniture and 179 acres of land on Herring Creek. I have a copy of that will.

Records show that Robert II died April 3, 1680 when he was only 29 or 30 years old (Maryland Indexes Marriage References, 1998).

Robert III would have been about 5 years old when his father died and about 7 years old when his grandfather, Robert I, died.

After the death of Robert II, his wife Sarah, apparently feeling that his affairs were too complicated for her to straighten out, turned everything over to the administrator, Colonel William Burgess, to resolve (Hall, 1941).

Colonel Burgess was an uncle by marriage to Robert II and also apparently a trusted family friend. When George Puddington married Jane Cornish, they had both been married before. Both brought children to the marriage. One of Jane Cornish's daughters was named Elizabeth Robins, and she eventually married Colonel William Burgess. George Puddington and Jane Cornish had Mary Puddington together, and she later married Robert I. This made Robert Franklin I and William Burgess brothers-in-law (with the sisters being half-sisters), and Colonel Burgess an uncle to Robert II (Warfield, 1905).

Robert II was evidently in debt at the time of his death, and it is speculated that a big part of that debt was owed to Colonel Burgess (Hall, 1941). After all was settled and the debts were paid, we do not know if there was anything left.

We do know that Sarah went on to a fourth marriage to a John Willoughby (Maryland Indexes Marriage References, 1998). Willoughby, who was also a land owner, offered to leave his land to his wife Sarah and then to Sarah's son Robert III if, when Robert III had a son, he would change his name to Willoughby instead of Franklin (Meyers, 2003). Robert III did not comply with that request, and we do not know if Robert III inherited any of Willoughby's land.

Robert Franklin III in Anne Arundel County, Maryland

*Th*ere is much documented about Robert III after he became an adult. He kept detailed records of his expenses and transactions and left a very detailed will of everything he owned (Hall, 1941).

Robert III (1675-1730) kept an account book that his family continued to write in for the next two or three generations. It is my understanding that this account book was turned over to the Anne Arundel County Historical Society a number of years ago.

Robert III married Artridge Giles (1680-1732) in 1697 (Barnes, 2009; *U.S. Quaker Meeting Records, 1681-1935*). Artridge was a Quaker. Robert III joined the Quakers, and the

Franklins were Quakers for the next two or three generations. Robert III and Artridge had five children (Hall, 1941).

Their names were:

- Richard, born in 1701 and died in 1761. We are direct descendants of Richard.

- John, dates of birth and death unknown.

- Jacob, born in 1702 and died 1773.

- Sarah, dates of birth and death unknown.

- Artridge, dates of birth and death unknown.

Robert III seemed to be a very good business man and owed no one when he died. He divided his 570 acres equally among his three sons (Cotton & Henry, 1920). Much of his land, if not all of it, was land that his grandfather, Robert I, had owned.

Robert III built his home around 1704, and several generations of Franklins lived there for many years. Although Hall (1941) mistakenly referred to this Robert as Robert II instead of Robert III, he did record that Robert called his home Oakland (not to be confused with the town of Oakland in Anne Arundal County today). Robert III's home was later called Boxwood. It was sold by the last Franklin to own it in 1941 and has since been torn down.

Robert III died November 8, 1730 (Cotton & Henry, 1920).

Franklin Family 1701-Present

Richard, Robert III's oldest son, was born in 1701 and died in 1761. Hall (1941) states that Richard Franklin married Eleanor Ward, but Hall's research stops there, and he states nothing else is known about Richard.

There is information that an Eleanor Ward was born in Anne Arundel County, Maryland and that she was close to Richard's age. On Ancestry.com, there are also Quaker meeting notes indicating Richard and Eleanor stated their intent to marry and were "at their liberty to appoint time and place" (*U.S. Quaker Meeting Records, 1681-1935*). However, those scanned notes don't include a date, and the meeting is listed as the Baltimore Yearly Meeting in Columbiana County, Ohio. It's possible the Richard Franklin in the meeting minutes is our ancestor, but thus far, we haven't been able to find proof.

Richard's will, dated November 24th, 1761 (*Maryland, Wills and Probate Records, 1635-1777*) states, "Lastly, I do nominate and appoint my dear and well beloved wife Artridge Franklin to be whole and solo executrix of my last will and testament hereby revoking all others heretofore made by me."

The way his will is written leads us to believe Richard was in fact married twice, possibly for the first time to Eleanor and the second to Artridge. For example, the children listed in Richard's will are divided into two distinct groups.

To his "beloved" children Richard Franklin II, Mary Norris, Elizabeth Carr, and Sarah Kemp, Richard leaves to them and their heirs "all that they now have which I before this gave them and no more." This group of children is clearly older, as indicated by the married names of the daughters.

Richard leaves one third of his estate to his wife Artridge, and then directs that any money made from the sale of the rest of his land should be divided equally among children John, Artridge, and Elizabeth.

To summarize, Richard's children with wife Artridge are:

- John (We are directly descended from John.)
- Artridge
- Elizabeth

His older children, possibly from Eleanor Ward, are:

- Richard II
- Mary Norris
- Elizabeth Carr
- Sarah Kemp

Richard's son John, our direct ancestor, was born June 5, 1750 (Godfrey Memorial Library, 1999).

John married Elizabeth Ward May 30, 1776 (*Maryland, Compiled Marriage Index, 1634-1777*). John and Elizabeth had four children:

- Elizabeth, born June 18, 1777 and died December 13, 1854.
- Richard, born October 13, 1779 and died sometime after 1850.
- Samuel, born February 28, 1783 and died July 28, 1852.
- John W., born January 18, 1786 and died in Sumner County, Tennessee December 13, 1854.

John served in the 1st Regiment Light Dragoons, Continental Army, fighting against the British in the Revolutionary War (*U.S. Compiled Revolutionary War Military Service Records, 1775-1783*). He died November 8, 1810.

———

John and Elizabeth's son, John W., was born January 18, 1786 and married Harriet Connor on October 26, 1818. John W. and Harriet had three children:

- Samuel, who was born August 4, 1819.
- Elliner Wyvill, born sometime in 1820.
- John III, date of birth unknown, but he died as a small child August 15, 1825.

Harriet, John W.'s wife, died June 2, 1826. After his son and his wife died within a year of each other, John W. decided to leave Maryland with seven-year-old Samuel and six-year-old Elliner and move to Sumner County, Tennessee to be near his two brothers who had earlier moved to Tennessee.

John W. continued to farm and, according to the 1850 census of Sumner County, TN, was farming 1000 acres. There seems to be no record of what happened to John W.'s land except for 155 acres that went to his son Samuel. John W. married his second wife, Mary Yaney, on Nov. 6, 1828. He died Dec. 13, 1854.

Samuel, John W.'s son from his first marriage, was born August 4, 1819 in Anne Arundel County, Maryland and moved with his father and sister to Sumner County, Tennessee in 1826 when he was seven years old. Unlike the North American Franklins before him, Samuel did not care for farming. The 1850 census for Sumner County lists his occupation as "house carpenter" (1850 United States Federal Census). The 1880 census lists him as "cabinet maker" (1880 United States Federal Census). Samuel made coffins during the Civil War.

Samuel married Jane Caroline Robertson in 1849 (*Tennessee, Marriage Records, 1780-2002*).

They had the following children:

- John Connor, born December 16, 1850 and died Jun. 16, 1933.
- Mary Elinor, born December 20, 1858 and died unknown.
- Nathaniel Thomas, born October 9, 1862 and died October 4, 1928.

- Hattie, birth and death dates unknown.
- Harriet, born July 4, 1866 and died December 16, 1934.

Samuel had inherited 155 acres of land from his father, but he and his wife sold the land to Wilson D. Turner on August 19, 1868. Samuel died May 6, 1886.

———————————

Nathaniel Thomas, Samuel's second son, was born October 9, 1862 and died October 4, 1928 in Covington, Tennessee. When he was 34 years old, he was laying railroad ties in Tipton County, TN when he met Elvira Elizabeth Lindsey. On March 8, 1896, Nathaniel and Elvira married. Elvira agreed to marry Nathaniel only if he would stay in Tipton County. He agreed, and they made their home in Covington, TN.

Like his father Samuel, Nathaniel was a carpenter as well as a farmer. In November 1903, Nathaniel lost his left hand in a sawmill accident, but he continued to do carpentry work and to farm. He built several barns in the Leigh's Chapel area of Tipton County, Tennessee. Nathaniel and Elvira had the following children:

- Bernice, born September 13, 1898 and died July 9, 1994.
- Will Ida, born April 28, 1901 and died December 30, 1938.
- Floyd Thomas, born October 25, 1903 and died Oct. 28, 1988.
- Frances, born 1907 and died 2003.
- John, born March 24, 1910 and died June 6, 2000.
- Lawrence, born in 1914, date of death unknown.

By the time of his death on October 4, 1928, Nathaniel owned no land and had no money. His children had to pay for his burial.

————————

Floyd Thomas Franklin, Sr., son of Nathaniel, was born October 25, 1903 and died October

28, 1988. He met Mary Oma Moore In Leigh's Chapel, a small community outside of Covington, Tennessee. She was teaching school at a one-room schoolhouse in the Leigh's Chapel community. They married June 15, 1938. Floyd and Mary purchased a 25-acre farm in the Leigh's Chapel community in February of 1948 and made this their home for the rest of their lives.

Floyd and Mary had the following children:

- Mary Neal, born July 23, 1939 and died August 9, 2011. Mary Neal married Gordon Domer Thorn June 3, 1968. Mary Neal and Gordon had two sons. Richard Franklin was born February 13, 1969, and David Gordon was born October 21, 1974.

- Floyd Thomas, Jr., born December 27, 1940. Floyd Thomas married Julie Alice Andrew June 15, 1963. They had two children. Thomas Keith was born May 25, 1964, and Julie Anne was born February 17, 1966.

- William M. was born August 1, 1942 and is the author of this book.

- Sandra, born February 4, 1946 and died November 6, 1976. Sandra married Jerry Eugene Honeycutt June 3, 1968. Sandra and Jerry had twin daughters, Tamara Leigh and Pamela Lynn, born November 6, 1972.

Floyd was a tractor mechanic and farmer. He died in October of 1988. Mary retired from teaching school, and she died in May of 1998.

William M. Franklin, son of Floyd Thomas, Sr., was born August 1, 1942 and met Patty Lynn Hayner, who was born July 5, 1941. William and Patty met while William was in the U.S. Navy. William was stationed in Maryland, and Patty, who was from West Virginia, was working in Washington D.C. William and Patty married on December 18, 1963 in Lexington Park, Maryland.

After William's navel service ended in March 1969, William and Patty, with two children at that time, moved to Covington, TN where William grew up. They built a home on one acre of the 25-acre farm his parents owned.

William and Patty had a total of five children, and they are as follows:

- William Michael, born December 14, 1965.
- Melinda Rae, born August 15, 1967.
- Tracy Renee, born February 8, 1972.
- Samuel Joseph, born March 4, 1980.
- Amanda Susan, born November 6, 1982.

After building their home on the family farm in 1970, William and Patty both completed college. Patty has a B.A. in English from Lambuth College. William M. has a B.A. in Religion from Lambuth College and an MDiv in Theology from Vanderbilt University.

Patty retired from teaching school in 1999, and William retired as a United Methodist

Minister in 2005. They bought the remaining part of the 25-acre farm from family members after William's parents died. William and Patty currently live in their home with their son Samuel. Samuel was born with Down Syndrome and has been a joy to his parents and a gift from God.

William M.'s first son, William Michael, was born December 14, 1965. While in the U.S. Army he met and married Dana Cir. William Michael and Dana married June 21, 1986. William Michael and Dana had the following two children:

- Joshua Michael, born April 30, 1987.
- Elizabeth Ann, born October 6, 1988.

William Michael and Dana divorced in 2005, and William Michael married Martha Horan in 2007. William Michael is an attorney who currently works for the school system in Salem, Oregon.

William Michael's son, Joshua Michael, was born April 30, 1987. He met and married Morgan Kylie Billington November 22, 2014. Morgan was born January 19, 1988.

Joshua and Morgan have the following three girls:

- Charlotte Muse, born Jul. 3, 2015.
- Willow Michelle, born Dec. 22, 2016.
- Mazikeen Diana Joy, born Dec. 3, 2017.

Joshua Michael is currently a school teacher in California, Missouri.

Afterword

We've reached the end of this particular line of Franklin family history—for now, at least. From Skipton-upon-Craven, Yorkshire, England, to Anne Arundel County, Maryland, to Covington, Tennessee, and finally, to California, Missouri, this branch of the Franklin family has covered many miles, both literally and figuratively.

I look forward to watching my children, grandchildren, and great grandchildren continue the legacy.

Bibliography

1850 United States Federal Census [database online]. Provo, UT, USA: Ancestry.com Operations, Inc., 2009. Images reproduced by FamilySearch.

1880 United States Federal Census [database online]. Provo, UT, USA: Ancestry.com Operations, Inc., 2009. Images reproduced by FamilySearch.

Anne Arundel County Maryland Judicial Branch: Sheriffs. (n.d.). Maryland Manual Online. Retrieved November 11, 2018, from https://msa.maryland.gov/msa/mdmanual/36loc/an/jud/sheriffs/former/html/00list.html

Barnes, R. W. (2005). *Maryland Marriage Evidences, 1634-1718.* Baltimore, MD: Genealogical Pub.

Barnes, R. W. (2009). *Maryland Marriage Evidences, 1634-1777.* Baltimore, MD: Genealogical Pub.

Beaven, Alfred P. (1908). Aldermen of the City of London: Bishopsgate Ward. *The Aldermen of the City of London Temp. Henry III - 1912.* (pp. 33-44). London: Corporation of the City of London.

Browne, W. H., & Dielman, L. H. (Eds.). (1906a). *Maryland Historical Magazine.* (Vol. 22). Baltimore: Maryland Historical Society.

Browne, W. H., & Dielman, L. H. (Eds.). (1906b). *Maryland Historical Magazine.* (Vol. 23). Baltimore: Maryland Historical Society.

Burke, J. B. (1858). *A Genealogical and Heraldic Dictionary of the Landed Gentry of Great Britain and Ireland* (Vol. 1). London: Harrison, Pall Mall.

Burke, J., Burke, B., & Nichols, J. G. (1846). *A Genealogical and Heraldic Dictionary of the Landed Gentry of Great Britain and Ireland, etc.* (Vol. 1). London: Henry Colburn.

Cooper, C. H. (1861). *Memorials of Cambridge.* Cambridge: MacMillan and Co.

Cotton, J. B., & Henry, R. B. (1920). *The Maryland Calendar of Wills: Wills from 1726 to 1732.* Baltimore: Kohn & Pollock.

Essex, England Select Church of England Parish Registers, 1518-1960 [database on-line]. Provo, UT, USA: Ancestry.com Operations, Inc., 2014.

Godfrey Memorial Library (1999). comp.. *American Genealogical-Biographical Index (AGBI)* [database on-line]. Provo, UT, USA: Ancestry.com Operations, Inc., 1999.

Hall, T. J., 3rd. (1941). *The Hall family of West River and Kindred Families.* Denton, MD: Rue Publishing Company.

Harleian Society (1880). *The Publications of the Harleian Society* (Vol. 15). London: The Society.

Lambert, T. (2018). A Brief History of Life Expectancy in Britain. Retrieved November 10, 2018, from http://www.localhistories.org/life.html

London, England Church of England Baptisms, Marriages and Burials 1538-1812 [database on-line]. Provo, UT, USA: Ancsetry.com Operations, Inc., 2014.

Maryland, Compiled Marriage Index, 1634-1777 [database on-line]. Provo, UT, USA: Ancestry.com Operations, Inc., 2012.

Maryland Indexes Marriage References. (1998). Maryland.gov. Retrieved from https://msa.maryland.gov/msa/stagser/s1500/s15 27/html/ssi1527f.html

Maryland, Wills and Probate Records, 1635-1777 [database-on-line]. Provo, UT, USA: Ancestry.com Operations, Inc, 2015.

McCall, F. (2015). Scandalous and Malignant? Settling Scores Against the Leicestershire Clergy After the First Civil War, Midland History, 40:2, 220-242, DOI: 10.1179/0047729X15Z.00000000057.

McCall, F. (2016). *Baal's Priests: The Loyalist Clergy and the English Revolution*. London and New York: Routledge Taylor & Francis Group.

Meyers, D. (2003). *Common Whores, Vertuous Women, and Loveing Wives: Free Will Christian Women In Colonial Maryland*. Bloomington: Indiana University Press.

Norfolk, England, Bishop's Transcripts, 1579-1935 [database on-line]. Provo, UT, USA: Ancestry.com Operations, Inc., 2014.

Papenfuse, E. C., Day, A. F., Jordan, D. W., & Stiverson, G. A. (2008). *A Biographical Dictionary of the Maryland Legislature, 1635-1789* (Vol. 1). Baltimore, MD: The Johns Hopkins University Press.

Peile, J. (1910). *Biographical Register of Christ's College 1505-1905* (Vol. 1). Delhi: Cambridge University Press.

Proceedings and Acts of the General Assembly January 1637/8-September 1664. (n.d.). Retrieved November 11, 2018, from Archives of Maryland Online:
http://aomol.msa.maryland.gov/000001/000001/html/am1--533.html

Tennessee, Marriage Records, 1780-2002 [database on-line]. Lehi, UT, USA: Ancestry.com Operations Inc, 2008.

U.S. and Canada, Passenger and Immigration Lists Index, 1500s-1900s [database on-line]. Provo, UT, USA: Ancestry.com Operations, Inc, 2010.

U.S. Compiled Revolutionary War Military Service Records, 1775-1783 [database on-line]. Provo, UT, USA: Ancestry.com Operations Inc, 2010.

U.S. Quaker Meeting Records, 1681-1935 [database on-line]. Provo, UT, USA: Ancestry.com Operations, Inc., 2014.

Venn, J. A., & Venn, J. (1922). *Alumni Cantabrigienses: A biographical list of all known students, graduates and holders of office at the Uni-*

versity of Cambridge, from the earliest times to 1900 (Vol. 2). Cambridge: Cambridge U.P.

Warfield, J. D. (1905). *Founders of Anne Arundel And Howard Counties, Maryland: A genealogical and biographical review from wills, deeds and church records.* Baltimore: Kohn & Pollock.

About the Author

William M. Franklin is a retired United Methodist Minister who currently lives in Covington, Tennessee with his wife Patty and son Samuel, on a 25-acre farm that's been in the Franklin family for seventy years.